T0208974

MEDITATIONS
on the
PARABLES
of
CHRIST

Peter Morrison

WESTBOW
P R E S S®
A DIVISION OF THOMAS NELSON
& ZONDERVAN

WestBow Press books may be ordered through booksellers or by contacting:

WestBow Press
A Division of Thomas Nelson & Zondervan
1663 Liberty Drive
Bloomington, IN 47403
www.westbowpress.com
844-714-3454

Because of the dynamic nature of the Internet, any web addresses or links contained in this book may have changed since publication and may no longer be valid. The views expressed in this work are solely those of the author and do not necessarily reflect the views of the publisher, and the publisher hereby disclaims any responsibility for them.

Any people depicted in stock imagery provided by Getty Images are models, and such images are being used for illustrative purposes only. Certain stock imagery © Getty Images.

Scripture quotations are from the Revised Standard Version, 2nd Edition, published by Ignatius Press. https://www.ignatius.com/Default.aspx

ISBN: 978-1-6642-3447-5 (sc)
ISBN: 978-1-6642-3449-9 (hc)
ISBN: 978-1-6642-3448-2 (e)

Library of Congress Control Number: 2021909839

Print information available on the last page.

WestBow Press rev. date: 6/22/2021

CONTENTS

PREFACE

I am still in grateful awe that my first book, *Meditations on the Holy Rosary*, was accepted for publication. Often, I sat at the computer with little idea of what I was going to write; I had only the names of the Mysteries to guide me. Ideas suddenly filled my head, ideas not necessarily from my daily recitations while walking my dog, Skooter. I hope this explanation will not reflect hubris when I say I suddenly felt under the guidance of the Holy Spirit. For this series of personal reflections on the parables of Jesus, I have again depended on the inspiration (quite literally) of the Spirit.

These meditations will proceed chronologically from Gospel to Gospel and from parable to parable. If, in a subsequent Gospel, the same parable occurs, I will refer to it with any new thoughts that may have risen since the previous version. As with every instance of God's word, no one can go deeply enough into the implications of the parables nor into their application for our times.

Perhaps my treatment of the parables should be labeled personal analyses. Possibly, my interpretations and analyses will echo those of bona fide scripture scholars. I have had minimal training in the understanding and interpretation of scripture; besides taking classes from scholars, I have tried my best to absorb homilies and lectures by the experts. Hence, I will be throwing the light of personal experience and of the events that have had worldwide significance in my lifetime on these analyses. I have been a teacher of literature on both secondary and college levels, and one university assigned me to co-teach with a rabbi a course titled The Bible as Literature, which was mutually enlightening for the rabbi and me.

When I was in my late teens, a psychologist told me I tend to "read too much meaning" into things. He then advised me to write and interpret on a professional level as a means of "regulating" that tendency. However, my tendency to over-interpret has somehow prevailed. I recall an incident in my mid-twenties when I and a friend were visiting Venice. I likened the Venetians to the pigeons that swooped down, not only on the Piazza San Marco at feeding time but everywhere on the islands, hoping to profit from the "tourists," such as we were. Upon hearing this, my friend exploded, saying, "Why do you have to constantly speak in metaphors? Why can't pigeons just be pigeons?"

His response made me feel like a pretentious snob, yet here I am, at it again. However, I ask myself, *Can one read too much meaning into Jesus's parables?* Of course, one may read the *wrong* meaning into anything in scripture; I therefore call upon the influence of the Holy Spirit in all my spiritual endeavors.

Come, Holy Spirit, fill the hearts of Thy faithful and enkindle in them the fire of Thy Love.

PARABLES IN THE GOSPEL ACCORDING TO ST. MATTHEW

THE SOWER
Matthew 13:1–9

M y first problem with this parable is as follows: if God is the
Sower, why didn't He avoid the path, the rocky ground, and
the thorns in the first place? Then I remembered that God the Father
worked through His Son, Jesus, who in turn imparted the word to
His disciples and commanded them to spread the word (plant the
seeds). Therefore, sowing the seed is inseparably linked to faith and
courageous action. It is possible to believe only for a little while, to
prefer worldly riches and luxuries to the Word. We can stunt the
growth of that tiny mustard seed, which should grow into a haven
for birds. The keywords associated with the Word as seed are "hear"
and "listen." Our ears, therefore, are for receiving the Good News
and listening (i.e., paying attention with mind and will to the Good
News). As for action, Jesus, in response to the cry that blessed His
mother's womb and breasts, corrects by saying, "Blessed rather are
those who hear the word of God and *keep* it!" (Luke 11:28, italics
added). Therefore, hearing the Word of God is distinct from keeping
it (i.e., acting on it).

Have I heard, listened to, and most importantly, *acted upon*
receiving the Word? Although I once belonged to a monastery and
was released from my vows and was allowed to marry, I now find

1

renewed meaning in the recitation of psalms and prayers. In that regard, I am following a lay-monastic routine—not exactly that of an oblate. Looking back, I remember that in the choir stalls, I too often concentrated on getting the Latin correctly pronounced, sometimes, for shame, in a spirit of competition with monks whom I considered rivals. When eventually we prayed in English, even then I fell short of finding deep meaning in the beautiful language of the liturgy. I concentrated too much and too often on pronunciation and the rhythms and intonations established by my confreres. After I married and had begun again to recite psalms and prayers and to do daily readings from scripture, I was suddenly reminded by the Holy Spirit that Jesus told us, "Not everyone who says to me 'Lord! Lord!' will enter the kingdom of heaven, but he who does the will of my Father" (Matthew 7:21). This teaching is not only a reminder to pray with heart and soul but to act as we have been directed by the prayers.

This parable is anticipated in the book of Deuteronomy: "Give ear, O heavens, and let me speak; let the earth hear the words of my mouth! May my teaching soak in like the rain, and my utterance drench like the dew, like a downpour upon the grass, like a shower upon the crops" (32:1–3).

The image of fertile ground, though more immediate to the time of the ancient Hebrews, is still with us in the form of gardening and farming. One of my neighbors has turned his backyard into a demi-Eden, with vegetables, fruits, bushes, and flowers. Almost every time I walk my dog, I see him planting, cultivating, nurturing, watering, and gathering. When his crop of romaine lettuce was too large for his consumption (his wife had passed from cancer), he shared a good deal of it with us, his neighbors.

Again, I am reminded of the mustard seed, which represents a *grain* of faith. Sometimes one sees grass or flower seeds, spread by professional landscapers, that have exceeded the boundaries of the soil and landed on sidewalks and barren shoulders. They have no hope of taking root. This, I think, is a symbol of those who, hearing the Word of God from pulpit, preacher, or reader, doze or drift from the monotony of words, emptying themselves of the capacity to absorb and to act. I too often find myself engaged in such drifting as I concentrate on the beautiful children present at Mass or decide what I am going to eat that day. In these cases, one must be continually aware of keeping the seeds enrooted through concentration and even a half-conscious planning of how we are to *reap,* as it were, these crops of God's Word in everyday actions.

Who or what are the "birds" (Matthew 13:32) that devoured the seeds? Who else but Satan or evil spirits? Most believers understand that the evil powers are constantly at work, trying to evoke the worst aspects of our personalities. They prompt us to make judgments, privately or voiced; they present us with salacious images; they urge us to hurt, insult, or misrepresent others. Worst of all, they provide us with convenient excuses. "Well, it's true, isn't it?" "I can't help it if I have a powerful sex drive." "He [she, they] deserved it [had it coming]." And while we're *calling a spade a spade,* we are in the grip of Satan, who, having won us to his side in a series of small victories, clears the path to future bad habits of thinking and acting—all of them justified by our lopsided egos.

Satan won me to his grasp in connection with my stepfather, until the Holy Spirit was kind enough to show me that I was defying, badmouthing, and complaining about a man who was trying his best to make a man out of *me.* For a while I blamed him for everything I was doing wrong in my life. Eventually, I realized that even my religious vocation itself was partly an excuse to flee from my big bad stepfather and turn to what I thought was God. I complained about him to the relatives of my deceased father, who pitied me and gave me tips for "dealing with" that "monster." Yes, he was an alcoholic, but if I were the least bit compassionate, I would have realized that his prohibitive upbringing, his service in World War II, and other misfortunes in his life were very much behind his drinking. In his sober moments—and they were far more than I realized while growing up—he held me to virtuous standards and punished me justly for my wrong decisions. The satanic "birds" held me prisoner in my resentment, plucking from me any tendencies I may have had to think and act in a Christian manner.

———————◆◆◆———————

"Other seeds fell on rocky ground" (Matthew 13:5). The soil is not deep enough for the seeds to take root securely. Perhaps the most intriguing words in this metaphor are from Jesus saying, "Immediately they sprang up" (Matthew 13:5). I ask myself what the difference might be between an immediate springing up and a growth that occurs over a longer period. In my mind, I see people responding to an evangelist full of zeal and emotion, calling loudly the name of the Lord and declaring that they want to be "saved." My guess—not to discredit true evangelism—is that many of these outbursts are driven, at least 80 percent of them, more by emotion than by genuine commitment.

I mentioned in my previous book that during my lunch hour when I worked for Grumman Aircraft, I would sit beside the runway and read the works of Steinbeck and Hemingway. Soon, I found Bishop Fulton J. Sheen's book *Peace of Soul*. The spiritual nourishment from that book carried over to my evening prayers. I experienced then what I must call a kind of ecstasy, whereby my spirit seemed to leave my body for perhaps a minute. I have no doubt that God was calling me to serve Him in a special way.

Shortly thereafter, I determined that I would become a Jesuit priest. The Jesuits told me not to bother, that applicants must *begin* with a background in Latin and Greek. Shakespeare had little Latin and less Greek; I had none of either. Eventually, I was accepted by the Benedictines, a relatively mild order. However, there were other things in my life God expected me to deal with before I could give my life to Him in a religious order. There were psychological problems, brought to light by a Benedictine psychologist, that would eventually cause a nervous breakdown if I persisted in that vocation.

Only part of the problem had to do with celibacy. There were erroneous patterns of thinking that had to be reformed by staying in the world and eventually marrying. Although my good wife has been patient with my flaws for more than forty years, I find myself still working to overcome them: disregard for the feelings of others; failures in responsibility; and as I mentioned earlier, reading too much meaning into just about everything in order to preen my ego. I was clearly not ready for the kind of commitment that any religious order would require of me. I believe that those moments of ecstasy were genuine; however, I needed to become more mature in the faith before I made lifelong commitments to anything except self-discovery and self-improvement. When I petitioned for a dispensation, the abbot kindly told me that I had joined without first having found myself. I am eternally grateful for his insight and understanding and for helping me present my case before the Vatican. I was laicized in less than a year and married within months after that. I supposed my Benedictine vocation to be planted in deep and firm soil. However, the rocks of my psychological state prevented fruition of that specific vocation. My mother put it best at the time: "You fell in love with a woman." That may have provided me with a simple excuse to be released from my vows, but I am discouraged from thinking that when I recall the possible dangers *for me* of staying in a celibate atmosphere.

Sometimes we do not test the soil before God plants the seeds.

———◆◆◆———

Who can escape the thorns of worldly concerns that choke the seeds, keeping them from holy fruition? True, we need many things that the world must give, which are essential: housing, food, clothing, and even talents that may be considered special gifts from God we must cultivate to serve Him. Stephen Sondheim, speaking through Madonna's character, Breathless, in the song "More" from the film *Dick Tracy*, expresses, I think, an all-too-common mentality:

"Each possession you possess helps your spirits to soar. That's what's soothing about excess. Never settle for something less. Something's better than nothing, yes. But nothing's better than more."

In his brilliant book *Following Christ in a Consumer Society*, John F. Kavanaugh refers to the "empty interior" of those who have lost their very souls in the pursuit of material gain. Consumerism, he argues, is a dehumanizing mentality, whereby we value ourselves only in terms of our possessions (2006 5–7).

Sometime the thorns are sharper than ever. As I write, the world has been struck by a virus that has taken thousands of lives and for which, thank God, there now exists an effective vaccine. Major cities are the worst victims. Many of those city dwellers have, understandably, fled to our village of Bellport where they have summer homes. However, the supermarket shelves are virtually empty. Perhaps the consumer mentality ("more, more, more") is at least partly to blame. The supposed security that wealth can bring, though not a fantasy, is plainly temporal, given the shortness of life, and certainly selfish. In a very real sense, the mentality of the acquisitive Romans was, to a large percent, responsible for the killing of the Son of God, lest He take from them their wealth and power. Devotion to the Empire and its abundant creature comforts dehumanized citizens to the point where they were dependent upon their military in lieu of their Creator. Of course, the Roman Empire eventually became the Holy Roman Empire, when Christianity was embraced by its emperor. However, once again the lure of wealth and power threatened to destroy the leaders of the Christian Church. Opponents of the Church blamed the doctrines and sought to create new ones; however, it was a *distortion* of the doctrines that caused the corruption, rather than sound doctrine itself. Pontiffs as well as papal representatives bended the teachings to justify their own avarice (see *Papal Sins* by Garry Wills). Martin Luther was accurate in his protests against the lucrative abuses of Indulgences; however, his solution was to condemn the Church itself and found a new religion, Lutheranism.

There are many thorns that would keep us from harkening to the Word of God, though we may be exposed to them in churches, prayer groups, and study groups. We might spend money excessively in travelling on the pretext of recreation and self-renewal. We may succumb to the fiction posed by "keeping up with the Joneses." This fiction is bitingly illustrated in D. H. Lawrence's story "The Rocking-Horse Winner," in which a preteen literally rocks himself to death to satisfy his mother's materialist philosophy and thereby gain her love. The story begins by alleging that the mother "could not love," not even her children. I quarrel with the notion of being born without even the capacity to love. John Steinbeck in *East of Eden* maintains that there are monsters born to human parents, such as his Cathy Trask, who is almost pure evil. Unless these are children to parallel "Rosemary's Baby," it's difficult to believe that God could be involved in the creation of inherently evil children. Only the human *tendency* to evil is present in every gene, as Steinbeck might put it. Those who act in cooperation with that tendency are, so to speak, throwing themselves into the thorn bush.

We must be vigilant, lest we allow the things that are not God to strangle our desire for Him.

WEEDS AMONG THE WHEAT
Matthew 13:21–30

The keyword in this parable, I think, is "enemy." It implies that evil spirits have successfully planted "bad seeds" into some of us and that these people coexist with good people and are doing them harm. However, on further reflection, one wonders about the evil "weeds" contaminating the "wheat." Two interwoven interpretations present themselves: the parable is not about the weeds choking out the wheat; the parable must be given a more universal perspective, whereby God leaves mankind to their own decisions, although He invites them to follow His way. The judgment to cast the weeds into the everlasting fire is not handed down pleasurably and without a forewarning I remember going on a retreat when I was still in my teens. I remember the Jesuit retreat master, whose name I have long forgotten, telling us that God *wills* the salvation of each human. Plucking out the weeds on Judgment Day is not God's will for us. We will have condemned *ourselves* by not adhering to His will. We make ourselves blind by saying, "We see," when we have plainly closed our eyes to truth and substituted corrupt theories, hedonistic philosophy, and opportunistic tendencies for the divine directives by which we must live, now and eternally.

Furthermore, there is no escaping Jesus's suggestion that His creatures can simultaneously contain both the weeds of evil and the wheat of goodness. As a child, I discovered the tendency to put my own comforts and desires above all else. My innermost being knew or at least sensed that I was wrong in my decisions, which were based on the self-deception of a spoiled child. Satan had planted abundant weeds in my soul. Looking back, I do not remember how or when God began to replace sinful tendencies with an awareness of His spirit working within me.

Some incidents are etched in my memory. I was nine years old when my father died, and my mother, brother, and I went to live in the house where my mother grew up. I lived there with my maternal grandmother, a saintly, religious woman; my favorite aunt, left single because of a distorted mouth caused by early infantile paralysis; a hardworking uncle who did his best to discipline us; and a grandfather who spoke little English and who worked as a gardener for a large estate. During that time I learned of Jesus and His love for us, shown by His death on the cross. Although I was still a selfish young man, I found myself talking about Him almost obsessively.

Even my devout grandmother, with her endearing Italian accent, felt the need to tell me, "Forget about Jesus for a minute."

I vividly remember my response: "I *can't* forget about Him, Nana." I don't remember the reason I gave, but I believe my obsession and my response to her was an inkling of the coming focus of my life.

It was the first awareness of a kind of vocation, though not, as I discovered much later, a vocation to the religious life. Throughout my post-clerical relations with women, including my present wife, I was part of the so-called sexual revolution. *This is what men do,* I told myself; *it is what my organs are for.* After I married, it dawned on me that, although I had given in to a male sex drive, there was no married "vocation" unless I returned to the practices of my Catholic faith: Mass, reconciliation (confession then), charitable deeds, chastity, and the care of a loving wife. This awareness of my obligations as a married man did not always inform my new vocational calling. There were still periods of a me-first mentality. Satan continued to sow the seeds of rebellion among the wheat of my godly inclinations. I now realize that I could become one of those weeds that chooses to be tossed into the fire. Therefore—along with millions of others, I'm sure—I find myself in constant battle with myself for a God-given field of wheat, free of fatal weeds.

The burning of the weeds will happen, of course, at the Final Judgment. I had an English teacher who became a good friend. One day he was discussing with us the colonial sermon "Sinners in the Hands of an Angry God" by Jonathan Edwards. He was visibly terrified and disgusted by Edwards's description. He said to us, "Maybe, as a Catholic, I have to believe there is a hell, but I *don't* have to believe there's anybody *in* it." A comforting thought. However, when one considers the visions of hell provided to the children of Fatima, the terror returns. Would Our Lady lie to them? Would they lie about what they saw: souls dropping into hell like leaves falling from trees? Or like weeds tossed onto the fire.

When in my late teens, I worked for Grumman Aircraft, and I carpooled with several other workers. They used to recount their sexual exploits on the way to or from work. Occasionally the talk turned to religion and the Catholic Church. I remember once interjecting a condemnation of the Church's teachings on hell. I said in effect that children of the faith are scared into behaving well by horrific depictions of the eternal sufferings of the damned.

The men surprised me in their response to my outburst. "No, no," they almost whined, in objection to my condemnation of Catholicism. It took me aback. Here were men who bragged to each other about their sexual conquests, yet they saw the Church from a different perspective than I did. Their defense of the Church then became, for me, a lesson in humility. I tried to be an authority on things religious, on fearful doctrines, but they, despite their sensual proclivities, were giving me a broader perspective. Eventually, I came to understand that however terrifying the threat of hellfire might be, it exists because we have rejected the promises of Christ:

not believing Him or in Him; not conforming to His way of living; not espousing His merciful regard for other humans; and most of all, once we are aware of the evil things we do, whether through conscience or the warnings of others, not turning to repentance and calling upon God's mercy. Hell is the consequence of willful "blindness." "Because you say, 'we see', your sin remains" (John 9:41).

The parable also contains implications for the tendency to judge others. A wonderful play by Lanford Wilson, *The Rimers of Eldritch*, contains a character—played by a teenage Susan Sarandon—who tells a woman (played by Rue McClanahan) who lives with an unmarried with a man, *"You're* the one who's going to hell." The play can be interpreted as a lesson in the fatal consequences of passing judgment on others. The focus is a man who is misunderstood and judged dangerous through gossip. The play ends tragically because of this mass judgment. Divorced and remarried men and women might ask, scoffing, "Do you really think I'm going to hell?"

If we are to avoid judging in these cases, we must answer that the judgment depends solely on God, rather than on us. For all those who violate Jesus's marital injunctions, excluding a church-approved annulment, we must pray for their salvation by whatever means God Himself offers them.

THE MUSTARD SEED
AND THE LEAVEN
Matthew 13:31–33

This "tiny" parable has many correspondences to the workings of Christian faith. Jesus calls the seed "the smallest of seeds." We know, for better or for worse, that something even microscopically small can have far-reaching effects. Diseases, for example, may begin with a virus invisible to the naked eye; however, they can spread exponentially from one person to millions. I refer, of course, to the crisis taking place as I write: the spread of the often-fatal Coronavirus. It may seem odd, even outrageous, to begin a discussion of Christ's parable with a reference to a virulent substance. I look upon the spread of a disease by means of a virus as the flipside of nature's ability to use the tiniest object to give rise to something fatally large. Jesus, on the other hand, uses the good things in nature to explain the good things that await us in heaven.

But how small may one's faith be, before it can become a "mustard tree"? What exactly, in seed parlance, is the potential kingdom of heaven? How does it take root in the soil of our souls? The answer is that we do not, cannot know, any more than we can know how Jesus appeared in the womb of His Blessed Mother. Jesus is not speaking here of good soil or infertile ground, whereby we either accept the word and cultivate it or fall away. He seems, rather, to be speaking of the kingdom of God within us, which grows until it has the size and shape of a saintly condition. Of course, the kingdom of God must suffer no moral impediments that could arrest its growth. In that sense, we cooperate with this purely gratuitous gift. We nurture its growth with kindness, assistance to the unfortunate, forgiveness of those who have wronged us, true worship and true praise of our Maker. The full growth of the kingdom occurs in the ultimate kingdom, where the "birds" of grace find a permanent, everlasting home.

The first sprouting of the kingdom may occur with an awareness. With me it was the realization of the little-to-no faith with which I picked up and made my own of the writings of Bishop Sheen. I can recall one of my first acts that seemed to combat the effects of original sin. I was playing a ball game in the street near my house in Massapequa Park, NY. The ball somehow landed on a neighbor's newly seeded lawn, and I walked on the lawn to retrieve it. The owner's wife, who had seen me through her window, came to the door to chide me and to tell me she would "call the police" if I ever trespassed on her property again. I resisted the urge to return to her a smart-alecky, self-defensive response. Instead, I apologized profusely and promised never to tread on her property again.

I believe she had braced herself for an insulting response, since she appeared taken aback by my sorrowful apology. She stammered and then said a quiet, "Thank you."

The next time she saw me in the street we engaged in a conversation about music. I had heard a piano playing in her house, so I must have mentioned the fact that I too played. Her husband was a composer of serious music and was in the act of composing a new piece. In the course of the conversation, I asked her whose music I should start with when I began listening to great music. She suggested Hayden. The next time we saw each other, she invited me into her house for treats, and her husband played a classical piece for me. Of course, I did not formally acknowledge these events as the kingdom within me, and there were (are!) times after that incident when I stopped its growth. However, God, through Jesus in His goodness, has always pulled me out of the abyss of sin, and my "mustard" seed, I hope, is on its way to becoming the tree of the kingdom.

———————◆————————

Leaven serves a double purpose in the Gospels and Epistles: It illustrates the growth or expansion of the kingdom of heaven, and it conversely suggests the spread of evil in the world. Leaven's or yeast's chemical properties have been explained scientifically as an agent that absorbs sugar and produces CO_2, thereby expanding whatever it is placed in, dough being one. (Encyclopedia Britannia) In its positive sense, as a metaphor for the kingdom of God, it increases the number of believers who hope for salvation through Jesus the Christ. Negatively, "the leaven of the Pharisees" (Matthew 16:5–12), for example, represents disbelief in Jesus as the Messiah, a disbelief brought about by willful blindness to the ancient prophesies and the desire for power and gain. In effect, Jesus was telling His followers not to accept what we today might call heretical and self-serving teachings.

When I was a teenager, my stepfather was anti-Catholic, and he insisted that my brother and I be raised Episcopalian, though we were both baptized into Roman Catholicism. In my senior year at Amityville High School, I went out with a devout Catholic girl. She was a member of the Catholic sodality, and she teased me about adhering to the teachings of a Protestant Church, especially one that did not believe in the real presence of the eucharist. When we were at the senior ball, she teased me about being a "black Protestant."

Fast forward, past her mother's scrumptious rhubarb pie and my "conversion" while working at Grumman Aircraft: one day I called the girl and told her I was "no longer a 'black Protestant.'"

"What did you *do*?" she gasped.

I told her I had returned to the faith in which I was baptized. From that time on our relationship took on a deeply spiritual character. When I told her I was thinking about the religious life, she was equally thrilled. Eventually, she married a young man who had earned his doctoral in physics and they had two children. I think it safe to say that this girl acted as a kind of leaven to raise in me any aspirations to the kingdom.

Watching the TV show *Catholics Come Home*, I increasingly realize that I am far from alone in returning to the Church or coming to the Church from another faith or no faith. Like the action of the yeast in dough, the kingdom spreads, swiftly or gradually, throughout those who are called in one way or another. But what of those who have not and will probably never be "leavened"? Do they miss out on the kingdom? Our Church teaches that they are saved by the goodness of their lives; that if they were properly acquainted with the faith and lived by its basic tenets—love of God and neighbor—that they have a share in the leavening. I believe this is related to the baptism of desire, an implicit desire to do good and an indulging in what we would call holy practices. These practices may include helping those less fortunate, forgiving those who have wronged us, and avoiding violations of what we understand as the Ten Commandments.

One of my favorite religious films is *Quo Vadis*. A Roman military leader falls in love with a Christian girl. When she is consigned to the arena to be killed with other Christians, who are taking the blame for Nero's burning of Rome, the commander is with her. He too has been condemned as one opposing Nero. Lygia, the Christian girl, wishes Peter (St. Peter) to marry them.

Before the ceremony, Marcus, the commander, concedes regarding Christianity: "It has proven good, full of courage, right here."

Lygia replies, "Christ is within you, Marcus. You feel Him more strongly than you know."

This, to me, is one of the most memorable exchanges in cinema history. (I am a film buff and have served in various film societies.) *Quo Vadis* is descendent of Cecil B. DeMille's *The Sign of the Cross*, which has an even more powerful ending, involving the martyrdom of both the Roman soldier and the Christian girl.

If one thinks about the Parable of the Leaven, one could easily find innumerable applications of it to the kingdom of God. One need only be aware the parable's depth of meaning.

THE PARABLE OF THE LOST SHEEP
Matthew 18:10–14

The Parable of the Lost Sheep has been somewhat puzzling in its use of the English term "little ones." I had always been a bit confused by the term until I investigated its etymology. At first glance the expression seems to apply exclusively to children. This is not the case. The term "little," as it appears in both Greek and Hebrew, can be a reference to anyone who is under the special protection of God the Father and His angels. The word appears in this context in both Hebrew Scripture and the Christian Testament. The injunction not to "despise one of these little ones" (Matthew 18:10–11) precedes the parable. Then comes Jesus's question, "What do you think?" in which "little ones" then become the "sheep" of the parable. The question presents Jesus as rather astounded by the fact that His disciples don't yet understand the full significance of the sheep. They are, of course, all of us, then and now, who need rescuing.

In a sense, because of sin, we were all "lost sheep," which Christ, in His redemptive sacrifice brought back into the fold. But to sustain the narrative, one must imagine one hundred sheep of whom only one had gone astray. Once again, we must shift to a universal perspective, whereby the shepherd is the Almighty, and mankind is the lost sheep. Essentially the parable is about God's infinite mercy and forgiveness and more specifically about Jesus as Shepherd willing to die for those lost to sin.

Of course, Jesus has not left any of his sheep to seek one who is lost. This reading would be too literal in nature. The emphasis on retrieving those lost would have had special significance for a culture that was so close to shepherding. Thus, the "little ones" must be made to understand that it is the solicitude of the Shepherd that is the main concern of the parable. How reassuring it is for us lost sheep to know that our heavenly Father wants none of us to be lost, to be left astray.

THE PARABLE OF THE
UNMERCIFUL SERVANT
Matthew 18: 23–35

" A nd forgive us our debts as we forgive our debtors." We mostly
say "trespasses" instead of "debts" when reciting The Lord's
Prayer, but how much in keeping with the spirit of this parable is
the use of the word "debt"? We *owe* God more than we could ever
pay Him: ten thousand talents, six thousand denarii, twenty years'
wages for a laborer. A large though limited debt? Surely the high
number is meant to symbolize an *infinite* debt, as in the injunction
to forgive one's neighbor seventy times seven times. In a way, Jesus
is forgiveness of debts (sin). He personifies that forgiveness in His
ability as the Son of the Father, to forgive all our sins, whatever their
number. We need only turn to Him, as the servant turned to his king
and pleaded for mercy. Interesting that the king forgives the servant
only because the servant pleaded to him; the king at first demanded
no recompense except the fervent request on the part of the servant.

God's forgiveness contains only one condition: imitation. The
Almighty Father is present in the Son, so that the Son may sacrifice
Himself in order to make God's forgiveness to all possible. *Now*, this
parable tells us, we must imitate the Father, the Son, and the Spirit's

merciful nature, to take it on ourselves, as servants of the Holy Trinity. Is it easier for the Almighty to do this than it is for those of us who have been wronged by our fellow man? The answer lies in the person of Jesus Christ, true God and true *man*. Unless it is "easy" to be tortured, mocked, scourged, crowned with thorns, and crucified, the answer is a resounding *no*. If we are unwilling to forgive our "debtors," it might help to contemplate a crucifix. Hanging there on the cross is the last word in forgiveness. Verbally, He forgives those who crucify Him, as He has forgiven Mary Magdalene, the woman taken in adultery, Peter, and many others whose sins He had forgiven even as He healed them physically. Would He have forgiven Judas Iscariot? Certainly, had Judas turned to Him and asked. Judas might even have forgiven himself through Jesus, rather than despaired and taken his own life.

Have I or anyone else been unforgiving servants? Yes! All we need to do is look at the many unforgiving attitudes we exhibit or express daily, among them hatred and cursing of enemies, homophobia, xenophobia, discriminatory organizations, torture, backbiting, and, yes, even "harmless" gossip. Television news, to some degree, encourages the tsk-tsk mentality of its viewers. How many of us, watching a report of some atrocity, breathe a sigh of relief that we are not like that, that the reported perpetrators should be killed slowly and painfully. The news, presented with clinical accuracy and a lack of any real emotion, encourages our feelings of superiority and our tendency to condemn others rather than pray for them. Occasionally, we get a hurried, unconvincing ain't-it-awful from the news team, but the accusation put to the media remains. "I thank thee, God, that I am not like the rest of men." In the words of Shakespeare, those who so report such outrages should "drown the stage with tears and cleave the general ear with horrid speech" (*Hamlet* 2:2, 562–63).

Only this morning I reacted judgmentally to a report from my wife's caregiver that there were people emerging from our local supermarket with carts literally overflowing with food. She claimed many shelves were empty of staples. My immediate reaction was to curse these "hoarders"; then I remembered that I have often given in to the desire, even before the pandemic, to take extra food, in case I need it in the future. Upon reflection, I ask myself: *How do I know these people are hoarding? Perhaps they have big families to feed.* I am incensed at people without knowing their needs, without "walking a mile in their shoes."

THE LABORERS IN THE VINEYARD
Matthew 20:1–16

The Parable of the Vineyard is so rich in meaning and in mystery, it is difficult to know where to begin. I will therefore take it sentence by sentence. The "householder" needed laborers. He himself "goes out" to find workers for his vineyard, presumably for picking, stomping, and storing grapes. He promises the first batch of laborers a day's wages, a denarius. This quid pro quo arrangement clearly refers to God and His chosen workers: Evangelists? Representatives? Recipients of the Father's special grace, the Chosen People? This is what I shall do for you, if you acknowledge and are content with my choice and my bestowal upon you the title of a privileged people. Herein, also, is contained a mystery: why *these* people, with an earth teeming with human beings? Why *this* first group of workers in the vineyard? One may as well ask: Why *this* man as prophet? Why *these* visionaries? Why *these* founders of charitable organizations? More pointedly: Why not those *others*, those seemingly *unfavored*?

Turning once again to films, I am reminded of a scene from *The Song of Bernadette* (probably my favorite movie about a saint). Bernadette (played by Jennifer Jones) is a novice in the Convent of Nevers. Her superior is Mother Marie-Therese Vauzous (played by the wonderful Gladys Cooper). Mother Vauzous states to Bernadette that she has never believed in Bernadette's visions of the Blessed Mother. Mother Vauzous has endured many self-inflicted sufferings in the hope of winning special graces from God. Why was she not favored as was Bernadette, whom she claims has "never suffered"? This question obviously tortures the superior; it is obvious that she wants to believe Bernadette, but she doesn't see in the visionary that quid pro quo, that suffering in exchange for special graces that is the basis for Mother Vauzous moral theology. If only she could see some visible sign of Bernadette's authenticity.

Bernadette's first response is that she does not know why she, who does not think herself worthy of the visions, received the grace. She proclaims to Mother Vauzous, "You are far more worthy than I."

Bernadette has been taught well the peculiarly skewed nineteenth-century understanding of religious life, with its emphasis on brutal penances. However, as Mother Vauzous begins to leave her, Bernadette, who never considered herself a penitent in the same vein as Mother Vauzous, suddenly displays the hideous cancerous tumor on her knee.

This revelation sends Mother Vauzous flying to the chapel to pray for forgiveness for "persecuting" Bernadette. Her words are a reminder to all of us who wonder about God's selection of people: "You have to be chosen; I see that now."

This summary of the scene from *The Song of Bernadette* is meant to bring us back to the why me? or why them? question. The scene says to me that God's choices do not always match what might be our own, or, in the case of this parable, our concept of workers' compensation.

In the householder's second venture outside his vineyard, he finds men "standing idle in the marketplace." The word "idle" in this context does not refer to laziness. It simply means "without a needed job." It recalls to me the many immigrants who stand in parking lots, waiting to be given jobs, usually in landscaping. However, in the parable, this second group could not be termed "cheap labor." The householder will give this group "whatever is right." Again, the casual reader might infer that the wages will be in proportion to the hours put in. The householder goes out three more times, the last time in the "eleventh hour," and finds yet another group of jobless men. The expression "whatever is right," if the householder is God, points to the incomprehensible generosity of the Almighty. It is extraordinary, beyond our ability to fathom it. In this context it means "whatever is right" from the point of view of the all-merciful, infinitely compassionate God. The response from us "workers" should be unquestioned gratitude, rather than an envious glance at those recipients who *seem* less worthy than we.

In the King James Version, the words are more pointed: "Is thine eye evil because I am good?" The second edition of the Revised Standard has the householder asking, "Or do you begrudge my generosity?" This attitude is tantamount to saying that we creatures are the final authority on what is fair and what is not. The parable makes the workers in the vineyard similar to the thief of the cross, the "Good Thief," the ultimate "Johnny-come-lately." Surely his appeal is what Jesus means when He says, "The last shall be first." The Good Thief is a "gate-crasher," with presumably no time in purgatory, and this is simply because "there will be more joy in heaven over one sinner who repents than over ninety-nine righteous persons who need no repentance" (Luke 15:7).

In this case, the joy on the part of God and His angels emphasizes the penitent, despite of how long she or he has persisted in sin. The laborers who worked the longest are the "righteous persons," but the penitents generate more spiritual joy. The householder is saying in effect that he loves to give to those in need, but he loves more giving to those who are less deserving in human terms. The supreme condition for receiving this grace, therefore, is the *recognition* on the part of the sinner that he is needy, no matter when he comes to "work." God does not adhere to our notion of time in His mercy.

THE PARABLE OF THE TWO SONS

Matthew 21:28–32

This a story about lip service. The one son said he'd do it, but he didn't. The other refused to do it, but he relented and did it. I wrote a poem about this parable.

"Two Brothers"
The brothers looked at each other with furrowed eyebrows.
"I had plans, and they didn't include raking leaves," Jake said.
Robert said, "Yeah, but we'd better do it, or the old man will take away car privileges."
"Yeah," Jake said, "but Sally is waiting by the supermarket, so I can't rake now."
And off he went.

Robert thought, *I need this week's allowance.*
The old man came to the front yard, and he didn't see Jake.
"He took off, Pop," the other said.
"Took off?" the old man said, his voice growing on the second word.
"Well," Pop said, "I got one good son, anyway."

"Yeah, Pop," Robert said, but when Pop went back in, Robert ran to meet his girlfriend.

I can do it tomorrow, he thought. And off he went.

Then Jake came back, with Sally in tow.

"Sorry, Pop, I'll do it," he said. "Sally will help bag."

Robert returned.

Pop was standing on the stoop.

"One good son," Pop said, "and one liar."

The liar set his jaw, waiting for the sentence.

The good son sat in the living room with Sally, his wallet full, watching the game.

Fortunately, or unfortunately, neither my brother nor I would attempt to pull a fast one on our father. We complained behind his back and called him "old Hawkeye," but he was a man to be feared when crossed.

Of course, the vineyard in the parable refers to infinitely more reward and punishment than does the giving or withholding of a weekly allowance. More specifically, the parable is an accusation of the leaders who turned the law of Moses into a reason to condemn others, and worse, to attain personal gain. By accepting the law of Moses, these men were expected to see it through to its fulfillment in the Messiah, as predicted by the prophets. Instead, they were sidetracked by the lure of power and wealth. The musical *The Book of Mormon,* however entertaining it may be, presents religion, particularly Mormonism but by implication all religions, as false, deceptive, intolerant, and preying on the poor. The all-too-prevalent concept of religion and religious belief is probably based on the headlines about abuse and generally corrupt officials. (These seem to be the only stories that make the newspapers.) Throughout the history of the Church, there have been church leaders who have tended to forget that it's all about "Christ and Him crucified" (1 Corinthians 2:2). A high school date once said to me, "It's amazing that the Church is still around, with all the stinkers it's had running it." It is still around, and despite corruption among its leaders, it's doing extraordinary work in Christ's vineyard.

Jesus proclaims that "harlots and tax collectors" will get to heaven before the religious leaders. He is referring to sinners who have turned to Him as their savior. no doubt, but those sinners He mentions are a reference to all sinners. The reformed sinner is one who has turned from his evil ways and once more agreed to work in the "vineyard," rather than in the streets. God's mercy, then, is available to those who return to Him after straying. This parable relates to that of the Prodigal Son.

THE PARABLE OF THE MARRIAGE FEAST
Matthew 22:1–14

G od is the King; His son is Jesus. The wedding feast represents the joys of heaven, the eternal worship of the Holy Trinity. Why then did those with invitations not go? We can gather from the responses of the second group that not only did they give excuses regarding worldly occupations, they were vicious enough to kill the servants who invited them! Jesus accuses Jerusalem of killing the prophets (Luke 13:34). This killing of prophets and the stoning of "those who are sent" describes a Jerusalem that rejects the "invitation" to the feast. Throughout the history of God's people, we find this pattern of rejection, and it was happening in Jesus's time, this time under the pretense of the Mosaic law. Was the cruelty of the Roman occupation and the eventual destruction of Jerusalem the means by which God punished the "killing [of] the prophets"? (Luke 13:34). The descendants of these men killed Jesus—God Himself. And there was a martyr before the killing of Jesus, John the Baptist. After the crucifixion, there was St. Stephen, the first martyr stoned to death for His proclamation of Jesus as the Son of God, apostles, Paul, and countless others.

Today, that which the leaders called "Mosaic law" has been replaced by the blindness of unbelief and the worship of materialism. We have not only refused the invitation, but we have denied its existence, and in some cases, such as in militant atheism, we have organized to fight the beliefs of the faithful. In modern, unbelieving systems there are holocausts based not only on religious beliefs but on ethnicity. We need only recall "the master race," the "cleansing" by Hutus, Bosniaks, and radical Islam. As in the parable, the excuses for the massacres were the need to rid the world of unwanted messengers who represent a life different from their own, exclusive concept of themselves. The "feast" is peace, unity, and love in this life and in the life to come.

The call to the feast may be considered constant, and all of us may, at one time or another, refuse to respond. I thought I was called to the religious life, but my psychological difficulties caused me to turn to marriage. Though I have been married to my wife for forty-six years, there have been many times when Christ called me *through my duties to my wife* to attend, literally and spiritually, to the marriage feast to which I vowed my life. Too often I refused the invitation in order to pursue my indulgence in the arts. Now, she is in dire need of my assistance in some of *her* more basic needs, and I too often put these calls off in favor of my "special talents." I ignore her legitimate requests of my time in order to play piano, read, or watch an interesting program. I find that when I let go of these indulgences and rush to her assistance, I regain the peace my selfishness has forsaken. Going to the "marriage feast" in this life often means to forswear other, mistaken feasts.

What of the guest who went to the feast but went without "a wedding garment"? No sooner was he in or at the door when he was "bound hand and foot and cast out into the outer darkness where there will be weeping and gnashing of teeth" (Matthew 22:13). Here we find a distinction between being "called" and being "chosen." All of us have been called. Some have not been chosen. What is the parabolic significance of the "wedding garment"?

I am inclined to agree with the explanation given in Biblelessons. com: "The wedding garment [is] conspicuous and distinctive, [and it] represents a person's righteousness. It symbolizes the habit of sincerity, repentance, humility, and obedience. It replaces the street clothes that stand for the habits of pride, rebellion, and sinfulness."

In Jesus's time, the reference is to those who merely think they are righteous because of their outer garments, with phylacteries and other paraphernalia. The tax collector in another parable (Luke 18:11) is properly dressed because he *knows* he is unworthy and asks to be forgiven. He is among those in the "streets and lanes" (Luke 14:21), who were summoned to the feast. O God, I am too like the rest of men, even worse, but forgive me and grant me a place at your banquet.

THE FAITHFUL AND THE
UNFAITHFUL SERVANT
Matthew 24:45–51

Jesus refers here to the politics of servitude. Here we have two kinds of servants: one who is solicitous for the welfare of those in his charge and is kind and understanding, and, conversely, one who takes advantage of the absence of the master of the house by treating his underlings cruelly and by indulging himself in the pleasures of excessive drink, what we today might call partying. The startling transition from cruelty to drunkenness needs a closer examination. I associate it with bullying, which takes place in schools and places of business. Bullies love it when there is no teacher around or when the boss is out of the office—assuming the boss is a benevolent one. Bullying and cruelty focus on the self, who feels she or he is superior to others and therefore has the right to be cruel. The drunkenness is an extension of that concentration on self because it represents an abuse of God-given pleasures. Drunkenness in a husband, who treats his wife as a servant to begin with, often leads to verbal and even physical abuse. The cruel man in charge of his fellow servants is a hypocrite because he has been assigned to care for his charges but, in the absence of the master, only inflicts physical harm on them.

In religious terms, he is a leader who has been assigned to love his fellow servants, just as the master of the house presumably loves all those who serve him.

God is, of course, the Master of all His creation, and those of us who serve him must imitate His love for all, especially when our "servants" are disadvantaged in some way. The unfaithful servant lacks this love and thereby forfeits a share in the love of the master. Whether the weeping and the gnashing of teeth occurs in hell or purgatory, the point here is that those who treat their fellow creatures with cruelty and disdain will somehow suffer a separation from their creator, which will certainly cause mental agony and probably physical pain (see Matthew 8:12; 13:42; 13:50; 22:13; 24:51; 25:30; Luke 12:28).

One can gnash one's teeth painfully in reaction to punishment, but one can also gnash them in an act of scorn for another person. When I was a child, if I were told to do something I did not want to do, I sometimes bit the tough back of my hand between my index finger and my thumb in defiance of my parents' wishes. By biting myself, I suppose, I was letting them know that although I was furious at them, I could only resort to harming myself as a reflection of the "harm" they wished on me. Such were those who ground their teeth at St. Stephen (Acts 7:54) when they were angry at the truth he spoke.

Leadership and love are inseparable; however, this combination poses difficulties for those in charge, such as bosses and teachers. My neighbor is an administrator and a rocket scientist, and I am a college professor. When we chance to meet and chat, we often ask each other how our jobs are going. He confesses that he often must stir the people under him to action. He is one of the kindest and most industrious people I know, so I find it difficult to picture him cruel in any way. My guess is that he successfully employs the combination of love and authority. I have learned, over my forty-five years of teaching college, that it is no good to square off at slackers. All they register is the fact that you are angry with them. There exist many ways to let students know you love them, *even as you remind them of their duties to the course.* Despite the difficulties of correcting with love, those in authority over others must try to do so. We must all be faithful servants, knowing that God, in His love and in His Son are the perfect combination of authority and servitude.

THE PARABLE OF THE WISE AND FOOLISH MAIDENS
Matthew 25:1–3

I often say to myself, "Christ can be here in the next minute. Am I prepared? If not, what must I do?" There must be a thousand ways to trim one's lamp. This parable of the wise and foolish maidens suggests that the bridegroom (Christ) commands us to act with the utmost prudence. He has given us the direction for our preparation: we are to go to Him, follow His way—the way He has detailed in the Gospels, which are the ultimate guidebooks for every minute of our lives. Has someone harmed us? We must forgive. Does someone need us? We must assist. Is someone hungry, thirsty, impoverished? We must relieve. The awareness of Christ in everyone is the best preparation for the wedding feast

This awareness, however, must be distinguished from what is known as scrupulosity. About fifty years ago, a coworker at Grumman Aircraft convinced me to go on a retreat with him run by the Jesuits at Mount Manresa on Staten Island, NY. The retreat master spoke of the dangers of being caught unawares, of procrastinating regarding prayer and good works. However, he cautioned against scrupulosity, which he called "scrutinizing our every move." A seriously scrupulous person is prone to suspect that everything he or she does is a sin. Scrupulosity places the emphasis on one's own fear of not being saved. It means regarding God as a tyrant, ready to pounce on the slightest misdemeanor. The problem is subtle in that it concentrates on the minutiae of one's actions instead of asking for guidance from the Holy Spirit in responding to each situation as it comes up. It is devoid of the joy one feels in serving God.

The parable is about identity. It asks us who we are, and Christ identifies us as His own only when we have believed in Him and shown it in our works. The bridegroom says he does not "know" the foolish maidens. Jesus has said, "I know mine and mine know me" (John 10:14). The bridegroom is telling the foolish maidens that, being late for the feast, they have lost their identity as members of the wedding banquet. Their lateness represents a lack of awareness of the fact that none of us knows "the day nor the hour." The keyword here is "watch"; watching means to follow in the footsteps of Christ in all things, not as neurotically self-conscious but in a prayerful attitude that acknowledges His constant presence in us and our neighbors.

THE PARABLE OF THE TALENTS
Matthew 25:1–30

I f one has enough talent and opportunity, one can become a celebrity and bask in the sun of public adoration or perhaps in the blackness of censure. The important thing is to be recognized, and some aging stars have resorted to lawbreaking, kleptomania and such, in order to retrieve the recognition they once enjoyed. Frank Sinatra is reputed to have claimed that he did not care what they were saying about him, as long as they kept talking.

Jesus's parable of the talents tells the story of money transactions, but it is also the source of the expression "God-given talent." We all received special gifts from God, abilities that distinguish each of us from all others. As St. Paul puts it: "In his grace, God has given us different gifts for doing certain things well" (Romans 12:6). Paul goes on to name a few gifts, such as prophecy and miracle-working, but all the gifts to which he refers are spiritual in nature. They recall the gifts of the Holy Spirit, given to us in Confirmation. The talents treated in this parable may imply physical, mental, and artistic abilities, but there are certainly various ways to enlighten others as to God's kingdom. We have not all been given the same abilities: some receive five talents, some two, and some only one. The different amounts do not mean that some are more deserving of the kingdom than others. The emphasis in this parable lies with the *use* one makes of the gift or gifts. The "good and faithful servant[s]" (Matthew 23:21) have invested their gifts and have received profits from their investments. The "wicked and slothful servant" (Matthew 25:26) has made no effort to capitalize on his talent. He should have returned to the master with at least one additional talent.

Why did the wicked servant bury his one talent? If the talent in the parable is God's grace to an individual, it cannot lie dormant (be buried). The gift, no matter how small compared to the gifts of others, must somehow be invested to cooperate with the grace. God's presence within His people needs a response whereby the recipient is making godly use of that "talent." To refuse to act on the grace is to disrespect the giver. It is spiritual sloth and a form of wickedness, as is all ingratitude to our Maker, to whom we owe our existence and salvation. We have all been given talents, and we must capitalize on them. Jesus is using the science of economics to make His point.

When I was in my twenties, an uncle on my mother's side scolded me for not having written a novel or play based on our family history. I remember his exact words: "When are you going to live up to our expectations for you?" I remember being flattered that they expected something so creative from me. On the other hand, his observation made me feel that I was not taking advantage of any literary talent they thought I had. That was more than fifty years ago, and, aside from writing a musical based on Shakespeare and a few poems, I fear I have not yet lived up to those expectations. Lately it has dawned on me that autobiographical novels are not exactly what God expects of me. My homilies as a Benedictine were closer to the talents I was given—or so I was told by fellow religious scholars and by the monk who taught a course I attended titled Sacred Eloquence. I have now begun writing lengthy meditations such as this one. I have a wife who is infirm, and I am not always as patient with her as I should be. Any talent I have been given for caring, sympathy, and understanding still has to be developed before

I can reap any sort of spiritual profit. I therefore ask God to help me realize the opportunities He has invested in me and to return His own investment *at least* twofold.

The kind(s) of profit God expects from His gifts to us is still somewhat puzzling to me. If the gifts bestowed signify our very lives, why would someone have more life than someone else? I believe the answer lies in the expectations that accompany the life. "To everyone who has more will be given" (Luke 19:26). Why did the master give five to one servant, two to another, and only one to yet another? Perhaps the "wicked servant" (Luke 19:22) was getting even with God, as someone has suggested. See the notes to this passage in *The Ignatius Catholic Study Bible: The New Testament.* I recall the drama, *Amadeus,* in which Salieri, jealous of Mozart's superior talent, wishes for the destruction of Mozart. This situation in the drama is probably bogus. The servant is termed wicked because of his jealousy of the other two. He therefore wishes to spite the master by refusing to give him *any* returns on his talent.

Tonight, I spied within myself the kind of jealousy referred to above. I am addicted to the quiz program *Jeopardy!,* and my wife flatters me by saying that I should take the test to get on the show. On this night's show, three champions were jockeying for best all-time champion. There are many categories with which I am only minimally familiar; however, one of the champions was quick to respond to every category, and he was usually correct. I found myself, like the character of Salieri with Mozart, wanting to see him lose, since he was far more informed than I. In the encyclopedic department, he was truly a champion. I decided that he was "smug" in his success on the show, but my pronouncement was simply an admission of my own inadequacy as a would-be contestant. It is never, I suspect, easy to settle for the talents one has received if others have received more. According to the parable, we must exercise the talents we have been given or which we have worked to obtain. It is so easy to sit back and envy. We complain to God about our limitations, rather than serve Him using whatever graces we have been given.

PARABLES IN THE GOSPEL ACCORDING TO ST. MARK

THE PARABLE ABOUT SEEDS
Mark 4:26–39

The development of seeds into plants must have seemed rather miraculous in Jesus's time. Nevertheless, our biological knowledge about germination should not lessen our sense of mystery regarding the growth of plants. To understand how creation works is not to have figured out God's hand behind the continuance of life in general. Somehow, the word *metaphor* in the parable of the seeds doesn't seem quite to fit Jesus's comparison of the kingdom of heaven to the germination of seeds. Of course, the "germination" of the kingdom within each of us is a spiritual rather than biological reality. Still, there seems to be something like a continuum between the natural and supernatural worlds. At the risk of sounding like a pantheist, I do believe that nature reflects—though it is not to be identified with—the mind of God. This concept is surely behind the idea of Jesus's parables. Jesus Himself speaks of the need for parables for those who cannot understand spiritual things.

The connection between going to sleep and waking to see the action of germination may refer to the fact that we have been open to the will of God and that God has therefore granted us the path to salvation. God may be said to have "planted" His Son as the incarnation of the kingdom on earth and that our belief in Jesus has made possible the growth of the kingdom within us now, the fruition of which takes place when we arrive in the heavenly kingdom. Jesus tells us elsewhere to observe natural signs, for example the fig tree, as symbolizing the oncoming day of judgment (Matthew 24:32). I recall that my Benedictine friend, before he passed from cancer, said that 2016 would reveal to each of us the sins or tendencies to sin that must be faced and reversed. I experienced what I consider the truth of that prediction. Suddenly, I was given a clear picture of the things I do, say, and think that are blocking my path to holiness. I was not "cured" of these tendencies, but I was so clearly aware of them that I could begin working on them through prayer and the development of habits pleasing or more pleasing to God. Among these realities I found myself too easily angered, too easily apt to hurt or verbally attack my wife, even when I had her health in mind. I laugh at smutty jokes and on occasion make suggestive remarks to my friends. I put important duties off "until tomorrow"; I procrastinate. But since my friend's prediction, I believe that the Holy Spirit has intervened to fill my mind with a special awareness of what I must do to fight "the good fight" and to "finish the race" (2 Timothy 4:7). This is the kingdom of God working within me, even as I sleep. I now live in hope that at least one leaf has appeared from this seed, which will develop, with God's grace, into a heavenly bush.

THE WICKED TENANTS
Mark 12:1–12

B ible scholars are quick to identify the owner of the vineyard as
God Himself and the servants as the prophets. The tenants, in
turn, would be the leaders of the covenant, those whose task is to
keep the faith as God intended. The word "tenant" is from the Latin
tenere, meaning to "hold" or "keep." This holding should have been
undertaken by the religious leaders throughout the history of the
covenant. Instead, they persecuted and put to death the prophets and
turned to idolatry, sexual immorality, and greed. Being faithful to
the covenant, which is a bond between God and man, means keeping
His commandments and listening to those "servants" who attempt
to get the Israelites back on a godly path.

Similarly, today's Catholics, whether priests, bishops, or laypeople
must try to keep alive the observance of the New Covenant, whereby
Christ and His teachings have set down the law of love above all
commandments. A brief look at the divisions among churches, the
rampant apostasies, the clerical abuses, and the murder of believers
should convince us how far from Jesus's commandment of love we
have strayed. People have said to me that they did not believe that
Jesus even existed, that the Christ was a hoax. Some have said the
Ten Commandments were not necessarily religious in nature but that

they made sense on a legal level, to preserve good relations among men. Add to these the vast number of atheists, both those who have rejected their Judeo-Christian faiths and those who never believed to begin with, and you have a huge portion of the population that rejects the message and presence of Jesus. Never, perhaps, has there been a more urgent call to faith and good works. To borrow from another parable: let us attend the wedding feast while we still can.

THE SOWER
Luke 8:9–15

L uke's account of this parable is essentially the same as Matthew's. I do find a small difference in Jesus's explanation of the parable. In Matthew 13:23, those seeds that fall on good soil will bear fruit and yield an abundance. In Luke 8: 15 "they are those who fall on good soil, who, hearing the word, hold it fast in an honest and good heart." In Luke, the emphasis is placed on *holding* the word, as opposed to forsaking it, and to maintaining a "good heart." In today's parlance, a "good-hearted" (Luke 8:15) person is one who is charitable, even to those who have wronged him or her. "Good soil" people do not only "hear"; they *do*. This, of course, is implied in Matthew (13:8–9) and made more specific in Luke.

THE GOOD SAMARITAN
Luke 10:25–37

"Samaritania"
A Poem

Drunk once too often, ejected from the shelter.
His falls on the street cause abrasions.
He sits on forty-fifth and Broadway beside a dirty box.
The actress who passes looks up to find her name in lights.
The priest is late for a dinner engagement.
The social worker is texting.
The man's abrasions are infected as he lies adjacent to his dirty bowl.
A teenager glances.
Stops.
Calls 911, and
Tells the officer that the man needs the ER.
The teen watches the man sober up.
The man released.
The teen buys him a meal.
They talk.
The teen proposes AA.
The man complies.

He is sober and working today.

And that is how one lives in Samaritania.

Have I ever lived there?

This is part of a collection of poems about parables that I am compiling. I hope the modernization puts across at least one of the points Jesus makes in the parable of the Good Samaritan: Those who *should* help their neighbors are too preoccupied with their own notions of purity and ambition to rescue the needy neighbors immediately before them. In the parable itself, the priest and the Levite are more interested in their legal purity than in the plight of the man who "fell among robbers" (Luke 10:20). The teen who helps represents the young man who sees past his elders' preoccupation to what is necessary.

The actress is symbolic of success, in this case theatrical, which can sometimes deaden people to the needs of others, or at least crowd them out of their lives. This is not to say all successful people are similarly unaware. There are many generous and socially aware business people and entertainers. Robert Redford, Joanne Woodward, and Paul Newman are three of many examples.

The priest, in this instance, is not living up to his calling. The man on the street may not be a parishioner, but he is a man in dire straits, and he needs on-the-spot Christian help. Probably the priest is well fed, considering all those dinner invitations. Even members of the religious communities can be sidetracked by worldly concerns.

On the other hand, Jesus's answer to the question, "Who is my neighbor?" (Luke 10:29) is not confined to those who have been robbed, beaten, and otherwise terrorized. The neighbor in the parable is one to whom the Samaritan "showed mercy on him" (Luke 10:37). The Samaritan showed indiscriminate mercy, since the man fell under the command to "love your neighbor as yourself" (Luke 10:28). The separation between Jews and Samaritans, at the time of Jesus, was itself contrary to the will of God. All people of all faiths should be looked upon as neighbors, especially those in need of physical and spiritual help. This fact is illustrated in the story of Jesus and the Samaritan woman at the well (John 4:1–40).

Sometimes, it is difficult to see people in the news or on TV as neighbors. It is difficult to extend merciful thoughts to white supremacists, lying witnesses on judicial shows, or corrupt officials in all departments. However, we must play the good Samaritan even to those who perform sinful and distasteful actions. Instead of visualizing them punished, in pain, or revenged, we must nevertheless see the neighbor in them. We must offer prayers for their well-being. Their present states may have placed them on the road to perdition. We must acknowledge ourselves as misled by similar false goals and longings. Often, we must identify with the self-righteous priests who uncaringly passed the victimized man. "Don't get involved" is the catchphrase of those of us who refuse to recognize our call to be neighbors, to the unfortunate, and even to the criminal. When I am tempted to watch trial shows, I sometimes share with a companion a spirit of mockery, often reflected in the attitude of the judge toward the plaintiffs or defendants. Add to that a contempt expressed as to how they dress or as to their hairstyles. If we must watch those shows, we must acknowledge these people as God's children and think kindly of them, no matter what evil actions they may have committed. The neighbor is "the one who [shows] mercy" (Luke 10:27), not the one who sneers and dismisses.

THE PARABLE OF THE RICH FOOL

Luke 12:13–21

"You can't take it with you" is not only the title of a famous play; it also reminds us that death puts a stop to many of the things we hold valuable and necessary in this life. The medieval play *Everyman* conveys the same reminder. In the play, Everyman, the character, receives the message that there is but one "possession" he can take with him beyond the grave, one thing that is pleasing to God, one thing that merits reward: good deeds. Anyone who thinks otherwise is the "fool" of the parable. The bigger barn correlates to the more expensive car or house. Excessive wealth tempts us to forget that there is only "one thing necessary" (Luke 10:42). Jesus is not telling Martha that it is good to sit idle while others work. Mary understands the necessity of taking time out to listen to God rather than always being "busy about many [other] things" (Luke 10:41). Jesus does not condemn the rich young man; He answers the man's question as to the *best* way to achieve perfection, the shortest means: "Sell all you have and give to the poor" (Mark 10:21). Even philanthropists, however generous they may be, are not encouraged to depend exclusively on their wealth, certainly not advised to luxuriate in it. I believe that the American dream does not translate as the right to make a pile of dough strictly to enjoy the good life. It is better understood as freedom of opportunity and the right to strive for a fulfilling career. This concept does not include the downside of the Vanderbilts, the Carnegies, or other families that exploit others to gain their riches. Not to dismiss the good that the extremely wealthy have done and still do, Jesus simply told us how difficult it is to reconcile wealth with salvation. I think of Disney's Scrooge McDuck. He loves money; he loves to burrow in it like a gopher, to let it run through his fingers, to throw it into the air and let it come down on his head. Funny. But it represents the mentality of what we used to call yuppies.

The bigger barn has, I think, a further symbolic significance. It represents possession of a greater area of storing worldly possessions. In this sense, the barn increases our capacity to think in terms of creature comforts but lessens our capacity to keep in mind our destination for eternity.

One last thought: If there are rich fools, can there be poor or middle-class fools? Given an expanded interpretation of the reading, Jesus is telling us to beware of any preoccupation with worldly needs and desires. He says explicitly, "Blessed are the poor in spirit"(Matthew 5:3). Although Jesus is not recommending the pain of "want" (we are told to give to the poor), the poor in spirit includes those without sufficient means who are perhaps more likely to look to their faith in God. The spiritually *and* physically poor may turn more devoutly to God, who has promised to alleviate human suffering and to reward "all [our] trials" (folk song) with a supernatural "barn."

THE FAITHFUL AND THE
UNFAITHFUL SERVANT

Luke 12:41–48

Among those in positions of authority over others are parents, guardians, teachers, managers, and bosses in general. I hesitate, in this era of women's rights, to include spouses. Ralph Kramden (Jackie Gleason) says to his wife in one episode of *The Honeymooners*, "Remember, I'm the boss and you're *nothin'*," to which Alice (Audrey Meadows) replies, "Big deal, Ralph. You're the boss over nothin'."

The authority of spouses over each other needs much qualification since St. Paul's words about obedience (Colossians 3:18–19). However, "sexist" he may have been, he emphasizes the word love (Colossians 3:19) in the spousal relationship. Both my wife and I reserve the right to be treated with dignity. Although we might (must!) act according to our sexes, neither of us should become taskmasters.

One of the most relevant definitions of authority stems from one of the meanings of the Middle English *auctorite*. From twelfth-century English, it can mean "one who inspires trust." A cruel and unstable person in authority does not, cannot inspire trust, only fear and resentment. The Roman Emperor Caligula comes to mind—a monster eventually killed by his own praetorium guard. Caligula thought himself a god; recall the story of his attempt to place a statue of himself in the temple at Jerusalem (Josephus). Compare this to Jesus's reference to His own "kingship" when He is before Pilate: "You would have no power [authority] over me, were it not given you from above" (John 19:11). God the Father permits good and bad leadership on earth, just as He allows His sun to shine on the good and the evil. The ultimate authority is God Himself, and the final reckoning is with Him alone, in His triune glory.

The uneven distribution of gifts may cause concern as to the justice of God. I prefer to think of the gifts as capacities to serve the Lord in different ways. God gave some a gift of speech, greater than those around them, but He expects returns on this gift in preaching or writing in His name. Such was the gift to St. Paul. The parable becomes more puzzling if one considers the fact that some people are born into a poor family while others inherit great wealth. Poverty, however, does not necessarily mean destitution, whereby people may starve to death. In this case, it is incumbent on those with sufficient or extraordinary means to save them from starvation. The requirement to give is not optional, if those who are comfortable are aware of those who are lacking necessities. Every day, I suspect, our mailboxes are full of requests to aid in helping to relieve those of third worlds. We need not reduce ourselves to bankruptcy by contributing to the poor (we may leave that to saints such as Francis of Assisi); however, we must recognize that God does not mean the destitute to die while others have enough or more than enough. For this reason there exists innumerable foundations to relieve poverty. To be faithful servants, we must exercise charity when we see others in need. This is the goal of the St. Vincent de Paul Society, to name only one of many charitable organizations.

Referring to another parable (Luke 19:11–27), we must ask ourselves, "What are my talents? How does God want me to 'invest' them?"

THE PARABLE OF THE
BARREN FIG TREE
Luke 13:6–9

I n this version of the parable, there seems to be hope for the fig tree. The vinedresser asks for and is granted another year in which to make the tree yield its fruit. Given the history of the Jewish leaders regarding the Messiah, believers may easily figure out the correspondences in the allegory. The fig tree is Jewish leadership. They have not recognized Jesus as the fulfillment of the prophecies, since they are waiting, in vain, for a military messiah. Furthermore, they are grasping and deceptive. The man who owns the vineyard is God the Father, who has sent His Son to prepare the leaders for the final judgment. The extra year for the fig tree corresponds to the mercy of God, giving His people more time to repent and to honor Him in His divine Son. But as with the renegades of old, the leaders remain "stiff-necked" (Exodus 33:3–5) and ignore the very scriptures upon which their covenant has been established.

The question remains as to how the leaders of the Chosen People could stray so far from the covenant. We must turn to the condemnations that Christ issued to the scribes and pharisees (Matthew 23). In Matthew 12:33, Jesus refers to the scribes and pharisees as "bad fruit." In Matthew 7:20, Jesus cautions His followers that they will know false prophets "by their fruits." The whole of Matthew 23 condemns the hypocrisy of the scribes and pharisees who, for recognition and worldly gain, have exempted themselves from the true law of Moses, though they occupy Moses's seat. They literally keep followers from entering the kingdom of heaven. The comparison that appears in the parable may also refer to any hypocritical religious leaders today.

It is with great sorrow that I remind readers of the unconscionable betrayers of Christ by the priests charged with sexual abuse of children. They are certainly deserving of arrest and conviction. Furthermore, they are to be prayed for and, through prayer and the sacraments, made to recognize and turn from their damaging, lustful practices.

Leadership in the Church today may be tainted by avarice and property ownership. Since these leaders claim, in Jesus's words, "We see," they will be "still in [their] sins" (John 9:41). The conferring of collar and robe and the laying on of hands do not automatically permit the unbridled actions of these people. It is easy to draw a parallel between the corrupt leaders of Jesus's time and those of today.

Will the fig tree produce fruit in our time? Like the vinedresser in the Gospel, we must live in hope.

THE PARABLE OF THE
MUSTARD SEED

Luke 13:6–9

The mustard seed in nature is exceptionally tiny, but once planted, its bush can grow to great size. Such is the mystery of the astounding growth of the kingdom of God, once the "seed" is "planted." But who plants these seeds, and in what way do they grow? I view the seeds as the small nudges into faith that God provides, whether directly or through His ministers, apostles, and saints. This impetus, if properly responded to with prayers and good deeds, grows to more frequent prayers and the multiplication of good deeds. I understand the birds that settle in the branches as emissaries from the kingdom of God, so that the recipient is already living in the kingdom. This kingdom on earth comes to full fruition in the passing of the doers and believers to the next world. It is a process more mysterious than the germination of the seed. Scientific explanations of earthly germination cannot fully account for it, except parabolically, in which God is the Great Gardener, whose methods are unfathomable.

Although I have occasionally blocked the growth of the kingdom within me since my baptism, there has always been something or someone to "prune" me so that the growing process could continue. Sometimes I lose track of the reality that we are all children of God and that we are our brothers' and sisters' keepers. Sometimes I disregard the feelings of others, either by facial expressions, tone of voice, or by simply asserting my own wishes instead of taking their wishes and needs into consideration. The kingdom of God needs constant attention since enemies from within and outside continually try to sow poisonous weeds into the garden of the Lord.

THE PARABLE OF THE LEAVEN
Luke 13:20–21

As we learned in Jesus's reference to the "leaven of the pharisees" (Matthew 16:1–12), it is possible for evil to spread throughout the people of God. This certainly halts the spread of the kingdom or displaces it. Without judging or condemning individuals, one can point to the new norms of a society that sanctions abortion, same-sex marriages, fraud, racism, and lying advertisers. Those who adhere to the laws of the creator are looked upon as barriers to "freedom." Nevertheless, those who hold fast to the commandments already have the kingdom, or its beginnings in them. The leaven of the kingdom brings joy in spite and because of the hardships inflicted on the soul and body. In this life the rising dough of the kingdom must be prepared for suffering in imitation of the suffering of the Savior.

THE PARABLE OF THE
GREAT BANQUET
Luke 14:15–24

The excuses given for declining the invitation to the banquet come from ordinary working people. Therefore, the parable reaches beyond the scribes and pharisees to include all of mankind, then and now.

My first question about the parable asks, "Why were the invitations declined?" I myself have turned down invitations to banquets, fundraisers, and ordinary dinner invitations. Those refusals I attribute to exhaustion, not wishing to listen to a talkative relative, or the desire to spend my time elsewhere.

If one assumes the "banquet" is a heavenly reward, what causes those invited to make excuses or at least to stall for time? One may assume that the "many" who were invited included the Jewish leaders, but I think the parable refers to anyone who refuses to recognize Christ and the rewards He promises. Jesus is speaking of worldly concerns that deafen us to the call of the spirit. Some are too busy for worship at a church. Some deem the priests, ministers, and rabbis hypocritical and even evil (think child molestation). Some turn away from the Church in a kind of spiritual laziness.

A priest and scripture scholar told me a story about a former parishioner he ran into on the street one day. The parishioner claimed to find another Christian church more satisfying. When the priest asked how the parishioner was enjoying the newfound religion, the former parishioner responded, "Oh, I quit that too." Church shopping may be considered another form of refusal to accept the truth of the one, true Church.

What might it mean to go to the banquet, to dispense with excuses and attend the feast? My answer must be faith in the promises of God. Those who refuse the invitation are more interested in property and marriage to put the kingdom first. Jesus is not saying that earthly concerns are sinful or negligible. He is telling us that all these concerns must be viewed in the light of the joy to come. Jesus said that being poor and being celibate ("eunuch" reference: Matthew 19:12) are ideal responses to the invitation to the kingdom. However, those financially comfortable and those married are not thereby condemned as refusing the invitation. Nevertheless, those *engulfed* by worldly concerns are, perhaps, more likely to forget the call to holier things.

There was a time, for months after my marriage, when my only concern seemed to be finding a job that would help us live more comfortably and provide better clothes, a bigger house, a new car. In the process, my spiritual needs were put on a back burner. We are comfortably retired, despite the illnesses of old age, but it is precisely the inevitable aging process that helps us to reflect more seriously on the "one thing necessary" (Luke 10:42). Acting on the premise that it is never too late, we realize that accepting the invitation to the feast (the heavenly kingdom) is not a one-time commitment. The invitations arrive daily, challenging us to accept rather than ignore them.

THE PARABLE OF THE LOST SHEEP
Luke 15:1–7

As I read this parable, I think first of the problem of alcoholism. For every alcoholic who attends AA meetings and gives up drinking, there must be thousands, nay millions, who have been written off as "hopeless" and to be avoided at all costs. Alcoholism is a disease, but it is based on a kind of hopelessness. The compulsive drinker finds temporary solace in the drinking bouts; these in turn lead to a physical condition whereby the drinker experiences acute withdrawal symptoms and is more and more dependent on the next bout.

However, there are organizations dedicated to retrieving these "lost sheep" (Luke 15:3). In the case of alcoholism, the addict must be willing to cooperate with those who would rescue him or her: first to recognize and admit the problem, then to follow the program. Alcoholics Anonymous is not a "cure" in the same sense that doctors' remedies are cures. In this case, the "lost sheep" must be willing to cooperate with the rescuers to play his or her part in the recovery process. The same may be said of prostitutes, drug addicts, compulsive gamblers, and thieves. What good person or priest worthy of his calling would refuse to work with them on the premise that they are sinners and must be exiled from their lives?

This, precisely, is why the Son of God took flesh: to rescue sinners from their abandonment to sinful, harmful habits.

My stepfather was an alcoholic. He left my mother to take up with another woman. Within months the woman called me, asking me to go to her home and take my stepfather off her floor, where he had been lying for three days. My wife pleaded with me not to go; my mother was surprised that he was living with the woman. Soon after, I received a call that he had been hospitalized. My Christian duty told me to visit this lost sheep. The visit did not set my stepfather on the road to recovery, although he seemed to have abstained long enough to stay with my brother for a few weeks in Virginia. Then he went to Florida to stay with his sister. She quickly decided that he should live elsewhere so she found him an apartment in another town. He called me from that apartment to tell me that there was a piano in the room. Again, I felt Christ calling me to visit the lost sheep; I told him I would go to him and play the piano, all the while hoping I could get him to AA. Shortly afterward, his sister called to tell me that he had passed. There was evidence in his apartment that he had tried to call for help. When my brother went down to retrieve Dad's car, he found the phone off the hook and signs of diarrhea and vomiting in the apartment.

I tell this disturbing story in the hope that at some point in my stepfather's agony, our Lord stepped in to call him to sanctification and that he responded positively. However, it is also possible that the drinking disease was just that, a disease from which he never had a chance to recover.

As the angel said to Mary: "With God all things are possible (Matthew 19:26; Luke 1:37). Christ came for all of us, but especially for his lost sheep, and in some way all of us are or have been lost in some way. I know I often await a rescue by the Good Shepherd.

THE PARABLE OF THE LOST COIN
Luke 15:8–10

The coins in this parable are obviously repentant sinners. What strikes me most is the particularity of this teaching. It focuses on one sinner, out of perhaps billions. Maybe, as with the thieves on the cross, only one of two. We are not permitted to judge others, let alone determine the number of sinners in the world; therefore, we are left with the rejoicing in heaven for one, *more* than for those who have not sinned. Perhaps I am thinking "too precisely on th' event" *(Hamlet*, IV.4.43). The parable is not about counting; it concerns the joy in heaven over anyone, anywhere who recognizes his or her alienation from God and thereby returns to Him. It emphasizes the grace of God filling the sinner and all who dwell with God rejoicing that the sinner has responded to that grace. Jesus is the great seeker; He has said that He is on earth to seek out sinners and to bring them to Himself, despite the objections of those who have appointed themselves definers and judges of those they consider sinners (Luke 5:32).

The parable recalls for me a confession during which I could not find any mortal sin to confess. The priest responded with a tone of extreme joy: "Thank God: *no mortal sins.*" But there were other confessions in which I had to confess serious offenses to God.

These were also greeted with the words, "Good confession." These confessions drove home the essentially forgiving nature of our Lord. The sacrament of confession, now called reconciliation, was instituted to attract, forgive, and rejoice over the repentant sinner.

THE PARABLE OF THE PRODIGAL
AND HIS BROTHER
Luke 15:11–32

"The Parable of the Prodigal and His Brother" stands as the most vivid and gratifying depiction of the essential goodness of God in His welcoming back sinners. It demonstrates, first, that God's relationship, His covenant with mankind is not a quid pro quo affair. Nor is Jesus saying that one may defy God's commands with the intention of returning to Him later for forgiveness. The story is rather an illustration of our weakness in the face of temptation and a realization that moral offenses in this life carry their own dire consequences, if only in the mind. The end of the path that leads away from God in the here and now will, sooner or later, betray the pilgrim "in deepest consequences" (*Macbeth* 1:3.126). The betrayal by these spirits of darkness may therefore be viewed as an indirect form of grace, whereby God is redirecting the path of the sinner through the consequences themselves. The acknowledgment on the part of the repentant sinner begins with self-abasement: "I am no longer worthy to be called your son" (Luke 11: 21).

The father's (God's) response is a reminder that the return to Him is not about our worthiness but simply about our wish to return. "Though your sins be red as scarlet, they shall be white as snow" (Isaiah 1:18). That is quite a transition! The blood that is implied by the word "scarlet" suggests self-inflicted wounds. The whiteness of snow translates as a state that transcends what we call a clean slate.

Christ's words to the woman taken in adultery, "go and do not sin again" (John 8:1–11) are also a reflection on the infinite mercy of the father. There is no denying the woman's offense; however, Jesus has called into question the ancient law that permits the authorities to stone her to death by reminding these authorities that no one is without sin and that anyone who repents, even those brought to repentance by the threat of severe punishment, may be accepted back into the fold if he or she promises not to sin again. One may assume from the parable about the prodigal that the son, having seen the consequences of his sins, will not sin again. However, even if he does once again go astray, he will, if he repents again, be accepted back with another "fatted calf." So too must we forgive those who have offended us "seventy times seven times" (Matthew 18:22), implying an unlimited number of times.

How do we imitate the Father's forgiveness? Do we kill the metaphoric "fatted calf"? That is, do we show our forgiveness by celebrating in a spectacular way for the person or people who have offended us and are sorry to have done so? I do not think so. This kind of welcoming back is the province of the Almighty. We are required, nevertheless, to give some sign that the person is forgiven and that his or her offense is forgotten. There must be a gesture of reaching out on the part of the one offended.

Since we are all children of God and brother or sister to our Redeemer, the parable of the prodigal is not only an example of God's mercy but a template to instruct us in our dealings with one another.

The depiction of the resentful brother relates to judgment and a misunderstanding of the nature of forgiveness. The brother exhibits what we would call a punitive mentality. Such a mentality may be created by the media, which reports constantly on heinous crimes. I find myself wishing appropriate harm to murderers, rapists, and organizations that defy the commandments or the injunction to "love thine enemy" (Matthew 5:43–48) or "love thy neighbor" (Mark 12:31).

This is not the same as God's justice. As the drug-addicted mother says to her husband in O'Neill's *Long Day's Journey into Night*: "I can forgive, James, but I can't forget." To forgive implies the attempt to forget. On the other hand, one may seek to remind the offender that his or her soul is at stake. This, however, has to do with a fervent desire to help save the offender's soul. I remember a priest telling us to avoid the mentality that emphasizes the word "me" in relation to the offender: "He offended *me*."

"Well, who are *you?*" the priest asked. "His Majesty?" Given our fat egos, forgiveness is particularly difficult in some cases. Some acts of mercy and forgiveness sorely require the help of the Holy Spirit.

I pride myself on my piano playing, though it is not perfect unless I practice it often. Nevertheless, I have been rejected as a piano player. These turnabouts have crushed me, and I became deeply resentful, telling my "woes" to everyone I knew. Furthermore, I became vindictive: I questioned the skills of anyone chosen instead of me. Thankfully, my hurt feelings gradually dissolved, and it occurred to me that the piano player chosen could very well have played better than I. Forgiving and taking back resentments can be extremely difficult. Jesus never said it would be easy, only that it would be blessed.

THE PARABLE OF THE
DISHONEST STEWARD

Luke 16:1–13

The ambiguity in this parable has challenged preachers and interpreters. The servant cheats his master to compensate for having been dismissed for wasting the master's goods, hoping to be welcomed into the debtors' houses by reducing their debts. One wonders about the contract, if any, that master and debtor had agreed to. It is likely that the master in the story was breaking the law by lending the goods out at interest. This master (who is *not* Jesus) has not met the demands of the Pharisees, whose greed prevents anyone other than themselves from capitalizing on their goods.

Yet the master "commended" (Luke 16:8) the dishonest former servant! He pats the servant on his back for his shrewdness. The servant was probably excusing the debtors from their interest and in a way blackmailing the master by indirectly threatening to turn him in to the authorities. I believe the key to understanding this parable may be found in the words "sons of this world" and "you cannot serve God and mammon" (Luke 16:8, 13). However, Jesus tells us to "make friends ... by means of unrighteous mammon. so that when it fails, they may receive you into the eternal habitations" (Luke

16:9). With whom are we making friends: the debtors, the master, or both? And what exactly are the "eternal habitations" (Luke 16:9)? Most probably, they do not refer to heaven. They likely must be accommodations the debtors make for the servant's shrewdness that is beneficial to them.

In what way, then, does Jesus suggest that we imitate the clever servant? Is Jesus being sarcastic? Probably not. However, He does seem to be saying that crooked businessmen and religious leaders who treasure wealth at any cost can provide a secular example of what believers should do to attain eternal life. I think of *Embezzled Heaven*, by Franz Werfel, in which a woman tries to assure herself a place in heaven by financing the education of a priest. The plan backfires, but the story has a happy ending for the woman.

Maybe "unrighteous mammon" (Luke 16:11) refers to one's wealth, gotten crookedly but given freely to the poor to merit eternity. However, Jesus adds a lesson about serving mammon (Luke 16:13). Serving, in this case, would mean a total dedication to making money, and, in the process, leaving God out of one's life.

THE RICH MAN AND LAZARUS

Luke 16:19–31

In this story, Lazarus is highly visible to the rich man each time the man goes into his house or passes his gate. The rich man cannot miss him. The lesson is clear: wealth carries responsibilities to the Lazaruses of the world. The destitute are hard to miss unless one doesn't watch TV, especially religious channels; one discards postal appeals without opening them, calling them junk mail; while driving, one ignores the obviously poor living conditions in some parts of the area; and one cites the poor and destitute as responsible for their own misery. This general lack of awareness and refusal to acknowledge the unfortunate makes anyone who is wealthy the rich man (called "dives" in other versions, meaning "riches") of the parable. The torments the rich man endures are meant to frighten readers; however, they can be quite literal if hell awaits the neglectful rich. One may interpret the plucking out an eye and the cutting off a hand as Aramaic exaggeration (Matthew 5:29–30), but eternal punishment, as Jesus refers to it time and time again, is real. In this parable, the rich man can communicate with Lazarus, which is probably not possible between the citizens of heaven and those of hell. Here the exchange is meant to drive home to listeners the consequences for neglecting the poor. However, I believe the damned must somehow know what they are missing in heaven, which would make their suffering even worse.

I have encountered people who expect the poor to "lift themselves up by their bootstraps," who say they are all too lazy to make a good living. The only way to respond to these people (was I ever one of them? No doubt) is to point out the plights of minorities whose opportunities were severely limited by prejudice or racism. The "excessive" reactions today of those who have endured discrimination for centuries do not surprise me, however nervous they may make me. We *owe* African Americans for having rejected their humanity for centuries. We *owe* anyone who has become poor because of the opportunities wrested from them. There are groups, such as the Ku Klux Klan, white supremacists, and, yes, the DAR (Daughters of the American Revolution) who reserve the right to ban entertainers (Joan Baez, for example) in the name of their concept of patriotism. Some organizations even reserve the right to kill people of color, people of the "wrong" religious affiliation, people whose ethnicity does not suit them. One wonders how many people have suffered hardships from the mentality of these organizations. I do not say we are a nation of "dives"; there are, I am sure, thousands of charitable organizations that assist the poor. However, if there is even one that writes off the "other" as unworthy, we can consider our nation tainted.

THE PARABLE OF THE WIDOW
AND THE UNRIGHTEOUS JUDGE

Luke 18:1–8

I t is interesting that the judge in this parable is unrighteous, especially if he is meant to correspond to God Himself. The story presents us with two extremes: the persistent widow and the atheistic judge. For purely self-absorbed reasons, the judge finally consents to vindicate the widow. The granting of the widow's plea suggests that if godless judges will finally break down with much pleading, how much more will God grant our persistent requests? The judge's motivation is the desire to be left in peace; God, on the other hand, desires that we do not cease to appeal to Him through prayer.

The parable asks us to understand Jesus's use of the words "righteousness" (first mention in Genesis 15:6; see also Psalm 7:11), "unrighteousness" (Luke 16:9). and "vindicate" (Luke 18:3). "Righteousness," in the biblical sense, means, first, to have faith in the existence and absolute goodness of God. Secondly, we only become righteous by acknowledging and accepting graces which *initiate* from God. We cannot make ourselves righteous. "Unrighteousness" means the opposite: to deny God and to do things that displease Him. The judge is therefore sinful and the widow in dire need.

Such vulnerability characterized many widows and orphans in Jesus's time. Throughout sacred scripture, one encounters the command to assist and to refrain from taking advantage of these vulnerable people. "Vindication" in this context means to defend and to issue justice to the helpless and persecuted.

This parable is not saying that if we pray long and often enough, we will always get what we ask for. Much depends on what we ask for. Furthermore, God's responses to our prayer take into consideration what He knows is best for us. I have heard of a prayer service run by a church. On one occasion they visited a prison and asked the inmates what they wished their group to pray for. Many of the prisoners asked the group to pray that they be released from prison. In the discussion that ensued at the group's next meeting, the prisoners' request to pray for their release was vetoed by some members of the group. At first, I thought those who vetoed the requests were being puritanical in their attitude. Today I think that a blanket release from prison of all inmates, whatever their crimes and mentality, is unwise. Nobody wants to be in prison, but some, I believe, should be kept from reentering society, if there is a likelihood that they would still present a danger to the populace.

To ask for justice, fairness, and deliverance from evil will not go unheeded by God, though the response may not be immediate.

THE PARABLE OF THE PHARISEE AND THE TAX COLLECTOR

Luke 18:9–14

The parable of "The Pharisee and the Publican," as it is sometimes called, has me quaking in my boots. I have an unfortunate tendency to imagine God being impressed by my "good deeds."

"Look, God," I say, "did you notice how much change I put into that beggar's basket?" "Did you notice that I wasn't amused by my friend's dirty joke?" "Thanks, God, for that ticket to heaven."

What saves me (I think and hope!) is the recollection of Jesus's words to His disciples: "Do not let your left hand know what your right hand is doing" (Matthew 6:3). In other words, offer your good deeds to God and then forget that you did them. Let the Holy Spirit take care of the rest. Move on, and *never* congratulate yourself.

The Pharisee is too aware of his good deeds; therefore, he justifies himself. He believes he has plenty of help from the penitent tax collector, who, he assumes, is beneath him in purity and holiness. It poses a spiritually dangerous situation for the Pharisee, who is not truly repentant. The penitent tax collector, like the woman who washed Jesus's feet, is self-forgetful; they appeal to God's infinite mercy and do not parade their self-justifying "good deeds" before the Almighty. Egotism and judgment of others keep us far from holiness. The Pharisee may truly give tithes, but they are ultimately unacceptable by God, because he gives them for his own self-esteem first. Worse, he judges the tax collector on the latter's reputation. A true follower of Christ would look at the tax collector and assume, or at least hope, that the publican is praying for forgiveness. The Pharisee should regard the tax collector with the eyes of a brother, rather than with those of a judge and jury. Jesus's condemnation of self-exaltation shows itself most vehemently in His accusations to this Pharisee.

The best way to avoid giving in to the temptations to Pharisaism is to keep our good deeds to ourselves. When someone tells us how much she or he gives to charity, it is with difficulty that we refrain from sharing our own charitable endeavors. We can keep silent about our own gifts to the unfortunate and, better, congratulate others on their charity. This is the self-forgetting Christian way.

THE PARABLE OF THE TEN POUNDS

Luke 19:11–27

"The Parable of the Ten Pounds" I associate with a passage in Revelation 3:16: "So because you are lukewarm, neither cold nor hot, I will spew you out of my mouth." The parable suggests that those who are committed to the work of God should be consumed with zeal for the proclamation of the kingdom. The number of pounds, therefore, represents the ability, given to all in some degree, to capitalize on spreading the good word. The "lukewarm" (Revelation 3:16) are the Christians who may attend church services but who in no way evangelize neither by their actions and words outside the church or by their participation in organizations that are devoted to evangelization. One might name them lazy Christians, who do the minimum. True, there are times when evangelization consists simply in acknowledging our beliefs for those who ask us about our faith. This acknowledgment might even be a mild form of martyrdom, since often our beliefs evoke scoffing and incredulity. Whatever the responses to our declarations of faith, the risk of mockery is always present for genuinely engaged Christians. Surely, there are thousands of ways to capitalize on our ability to promote the faith. The lukewarm, fearful, embarrassed servant turns her or his back on all opportunities for evangelization. This tepidness is understandably associated with expectoration and vomiting.

Then there are those who have withdrawn from the faith because of a tragedy in their lives: the loss of a parent, the death of a child, sexual abuse from a clergyman. Often, I believe, God permits these evils, not to make us give up on Him but to help us to follow the way of the cross. Some of those who have suffered have posed a common question: "If God is so good, why would He not prevent these tragedies?" Though we do not at present know of the reasons for God's allowing these evils to occur, our belief in Him must include acknowledgment of our imperfect earthly existence, and most of all, trust in the presence and absolute goodness of the Almighty, who "makes His sun rise on the evil and on the good" (Matthew 5:45).

THE PARABLE OF THE
WICKED TENANTS

Luke 20:9–18

The nobleman of the parable may be God the Father (Luke 20:9). However, his going into another country to obtain kingly power seems mystifying. Isn't God the Father all-powerful to begin with? On closer scrutiny, God's "another country" (Luke 20:9) could stand for his keeping Himself hidden until He revealed Himself to the ancient Israelites, who are the tenants (Luke 20:9). Not only did God reveal Himself, He adopted them, made them His own special people. It was the job of the "tenants" to keep His name alive and to take care of the vineyard that it might work to produce more believers and discourage belief in false gods. The people God sends to bring back the "fruit" (Luke 20:10) of His labors are the prophets, who find, instead of fidelity to the one true God, a betrayal whereby God's people have gone to pagan gods. When the servants (prophets) remind the transgressors of their idolatry, they are killed. When the parable speaks of the son (Luke 20:13), it is referring to Jesus. At the time of Jesus's coming, the leaders of the Israelites were so inured to ignoring and killing the prophets that anyone who threatened their practices and beliefs was in danger of torture and death. The leaders in Jesus's time were given many opportunities to acknowledge Christ as the Messiah: the miracles, the teachings based on scripture, the fulfillment of the prophecies regarding the sacrificial Lamb of God (Micah 5:2; Psalm 22:7–8, 16–18; Isaiah 53:5; Isaiah 53:7). They chose to ignore their own heritage for the sake of power and gain. Destroying the "tenants" (Luke 20:16) no doubt refers to the destruction of Jerusalem and its temple. The corrupt leaders say, "We see" (John 9:41), and they are therefore left in their blindness. The "others" (Luke 20:16), to whom the vineyard will be given, denotes gentiles and any Jew, such as Paul, who, albeit through supernatural means, comes to believe in Jesus, rather than persecute His followers (Acts 9:3–9).

EPILOGUE

Further Thoughts on the Parables

Considering the God-Man who taught in parables, our understanding and interpretation of them invites ever deeper enlightenment and application of their messages to our own lives and time. I will therefore list the thoughts that have come to me since the above reflections.

The parables are rich in their implications, which recall the words of Christ to the Samaritan woman at the well concerning the eternal well (John 4:13–14). These stories serve as ongoing standards against which to set our thoughts, actions, and decisions. Together they ask us to acknowledge Jesus and His teachings as the only "door" (John 10: 1) to the fold, the ultimate judge of our beliefs, thoughts, and actions.

Jesus's constant use of nature gives a special role to the natural: they become reflections of the world of the supernatural. Thus, one might say that nature, though fallen, is somehow sacralized.

Mercy and forgiveness constitute the constant themes of the parables. Not to acknowledge these graces is to risk condemnation, since by our refusal we say we do not consider ourselves sinful. To ask for forgiveness is to admit that we have done something to forgive. Sin is our condition, both original and actual, whether we acknowledge them or not. God wants us to admit guilt and then turn to Him for infinite mercy. He goes out of His way as the divine Shepherd to find the lost sheep (souls) and bring them back to the fold (John 10:16).

His methods for retrieving souls are manifold. Often, He allows a crisis in our lives to awaken us to the need for redemption. Sometimes it is our respect for someone who models belief and repentance. It might be a natural phenomenon, such as lethal weather conditions, a disease, or a pandemic such as we are experiencing as I write. Regarding the latter, it may be my imagination working overtime, but it seems to me that people I encounter on the streets, in stores, and among neighbors are more than ever attentive to our dispositions, our need for smiles, encouragement, and sharing hopeful thoughts. This morning I drove to a bakery to buy cheese Danishes for my wife. A woman coming out of the bakery, whom I did not know, took time to have a brief chat with me about the weather. People driving and walking down our scenic street almost inevitably exchange pleasantries. I believe I know the names and breeds of dogs for miles around. As a radio disc jockey from my youth (Ted Brown) used to say, "The hostility index is considerably low today."

I recall Dietrich Von Hildebrand, in his book *Transformation in Christ*, advising Christians to be sponge-like when receiving insults and other forms of harm. The true Christian does not return insult for insult nor seek to exact revenge for harm from others. He does not mean that we should offer no line of defense, but that it should not be in kind. If someone elects to pound my head, I would be obliged to cover my head, lest the blows damage my brain. Self-defense is not synonymous with retaliation.

The parables emphasize the unfathomable mercy to our God, which reaches out to the penitent. Once in the confessional, I told the priest that my feelings of guilt for previous acts—from which I had been absolved—caused me ongoing grievance. The priest pointed out an important distinction between actual guilt and what he termed "emotional guilt." The latter, I believe, is called compunction, whereby we always regret our offenses to God but are confident that He has forgiven us. Moreover, I know that even though I have been forgiven for my offenses, I have made myself weak in certain areas. Jesus's words to the woman taken in adultery, "Woman, go and leave your life of sin" (John 8:11) probably resonated with her as a difficult task, a habit hard to break. I know that I have made myself weak against the temptations of the flesh and must constantly fight to stay guiltless—if indeed I am!

Responding positively to God is to make possible the growth of the mustard seed (Matthew 17:20), the action of the leaven (Matthew 16:1–12), and the unhampered growth of the wheat (Matthew 13:24). The seed falls only on rich soil (Matthew 13:23). The woman finds her lost coin (Luke 15:8–10).

The mercy of God is always before us, but He wants us to persist in our requests for it (Luke 18:1–8).

The judgment forbidden to us in the parables is that which presumes to know God's mind regarding the apparent wrongdoing of our neighbors (Luke 18:9–14).

When we hear the call to evangelize, we must not stand there idle but use every means in our power to spread the Good News (Matthew 20:6).

Lord, in all my decisions, thoughts, actions, and words, let me be mindful of Your will and of our eternal destinies. Amen.

Printed in the United States
by Baker & Taylor Publisher Services